Yes, the Ducks Were Real

Yes, the Ducks Were Real

Poems

Linda Lerner

The New York Quarterly Foundation, Inc.
New York, New York

NYQ Books™ is an imprint of The New York Quarterly Foundation, Inc.

The New York Quarterly Foundation, Inc.
P. O. Box 2015
Old Chelsea Station
New York, NY 10113

www.nyq.org

Copyright © 2015 by Linda Lerner

All rights reserved. No part of this book may be used or reproduced in any manner whatsoever without written permission of the author except in the case of brief quotations embodied in critical articles and reviews.

First Edition

Set in New Baskerville

Layout by Christina Sinibaldi

Cover Design by Raymond P. Hammond

Cover Illustration: "Wilderness," 14x16", acrylic on canvas, 2014 by Angela Mark and Michael Shores, Sharkart Studios
www.sharkartstudios.com

Library of Congress Control Number: 2015930650

ISBN: 978-1-935520-86-3

Yes, the Ducks Were Real

ACKNOWLEDGMENTS

Grateful acknowledgment is made to the following journals in which these poems first appeared:

"Those Poems Like Safe Houses" appeared in *Big Hammer*. The following six poems appeared in *New Verse News*: "Dire Warnings," "Those Looking Down: Watch Listen," "Unfinished," "Shoveling," "Sneaking Across the Border," and "A Terrible Beauty." "Two Words" appeared in *The Mom Egg*. "The Storm" appeared in the anthology, *Songs of Sandy*. "On Trying to Understand What It Means to Owe Trillions" appeared in *Lummox*. "Hologram" and "With Grateful Acknowledgment to Wallace Stevens" appeared in *Two Bridges*. "Thumbing a Ride" appeared in *Gutter Eloquence*. The following two poems, "Like Any Drunkard" and "My Name Rings in the New Year," appeared in *Nomad's Choir*. "Listening to *The Trapeze Performers* by Matisse" appeared in *Maintenant*. "The Starting Gate" appeared in the anthology *At the Gate: Departures & Arrivals*. "Stand Down" appeared in *Poetrymag.com*. "The Girls from Hell Come to Collect" appeared in *Lips*. The following four poems appeared in *Acoustic Levitation:* "Young Man With a Guitar," "Without Sound or Sense," "42nd Street on a Saturday Night," and "Like Any Drunkard." "Whenever & Always" appeared in *First Literary Review East*. The following five poems appeared in *Danse Macabre:* "Lost in a Comic Trying to Be a Graphic Novel," "Saint in a Sardine Can," "Ring Around the Rosy," "What Just Happened" and "On Visiting MoMA," which appears in this collection as "Three Exhibits: Inventing Abstraction, 1910—1925." "The Missing Key" appeared in *Chronogram*. "What Is the Where" appeared in *Maintenant*. "On Diego Rivera" appeared in *Dinner with the Muse*. "Halloween 2008" appeared in *Home Planet News*. The following poems appeared in *Rusty Truck:* "Stand Down," "The System," "It's Because," "A Day Like Any Other," and "Ex Wives Caught in the Jam." "A Stand-in for Zelda" appeared in *Brownstone Poets*. "Call Him Pegasus" appeared in *Rockhurt Review*. "What About the Fish?" appeared in *Van Gogh's Ear*. "There's No Stopping It" appeared in *Onthebus*. "Who Dares Invoke the Bard" appeared in *Chiron Review*. "Saint in a Sardine Can" appeared in *Danse Macabre*. "Snowlight" appeared in *Poetry Bay*. "Crossing Lines" appeared in the column "Walt's Corner" in the *The Long Islander*. "Stumbling on Jack's Road" appeared in *Gutter Eloquence*. "It's the Blues," appeared in *Up the Staircase Quarterly*. "Fear As Loud as a Mugging" appeared in *The five Two: Crime Poetry Weekly*."Ring Around the Rosey" and "Stumbling on Jack's Road" appeared in *Ding Dong the Bell Pussy in the Well*, Lummox Press, 2014.

Contents

I—The Girls from Hell Come to Collect

The Girls from Hell Come to Collect / 13
Stumbling on Jack's Road / 14
It's the Kid / 15
For Women: When Then Is Now / 16
It's a Road That Goes Straight Ahead in a Circle Straight
    Ahead / 17
The Thing About Blame / 18
Lost in a Comic Trying to Be a Graphic Novel / 20
Two Photos / 22
For the Promised Elixir of Immortal Health a Friend Tells
    Me To / 24
Giving Thanks / 25
The Inevitability of What's Random Or / 26
An Old Wive's Tale or a Rip Van Winkle Story / 27
Long Hot Summer / 28
October's Trick / 29
My Name Rings in the New Year / 30
Going Somewhere Who's Going Somewhere / 31
September Poem / 33

II—The Missing Key: U

Yes, the Ducks Were Real / 37
The Missing Key: U / 40
Crossing Lines / 41
Summer Solstice / 42
Whenever and Always / 43
Unfinished / 44
An Apple Isn't a Peach / 45
Two Words / 46

Halloween, 2008 / 47
Snowlight / 48
In the Terrible Final Months of 2012 / 49
Off the Record / 50
42nd Street on a Saturday Night / 51
Ex Wives Caught in the Jam / 52
The Starting Gate / 53
Call Him Pegasus / 54

III—Matisse Poems

Almost Naked / 57
Matisse's Version Versus Mine / 58
Nobody & Nothing / 59
Listening to *The Trapeze Performers* by Matisse / 60
The Caption Reads: *Madame Matisse with Manila Shawl* / 61
The Family / 63

IV—To Those Looking Down...

To Those Looking Down: Watch, Listen / 67
A Terrible Beauty / 69
Those Poems Like Safe Houses / 70
Stand Down / 71
A Roach Poem / 72
Shoveling / 73
The Storm / 75
Dire Warnings / 76
On Trying to Understand What It Means to Owe Trillions, What a Trillion Even Is / 77
No Flowers for Terrorists, a Cry for Peace / 78
It's Because / 80
Thumbing a Ride / 81

The Invasion   / 82
Sneaking Across the Border   / 83
What About the Fish?   / 84
The System   / 85
Drives thru a Poem Like He's Headed for That Cliff He's
    Been Over Before   / 86

V—Without Sound or Sense

Without Sound or Sense   / 91
In the Company of Nice People I Keep Quiet   / 92
"What Is the Where?"   / 93
Like Any Drunkard   / 94
It's the Blues   / 95
On Hearing the James Singleton Quartet   / 96
Me, Punk and Lou Reed   / 97
For Iris Berman   / 99
There's No Stopping It   / 100
New York Winter, 2012   / 102
With Grateful Acknowledgment to Wallace Stevens   / 103
Three Exhibits: Inventing Abstraction, 1910—1925   / 104
Young Man with a Guitar   / 105
Fear as Loud as a Mugging   / 106
On a Flight Hijacked by Diego Rivera   / 107
On Diego Rivera   / 108
Saint in a Sardine Can   / 109
Who Dares Invoke the Bard?   / 110
Two Bombs   / 111

I—The Girls from Hell Come to Collect

The Girls from Hell Come to Collect

listen hard and
you'll hear the raw of motorcycles in their voices
see them riding on the back of a harley
flying high above lives nobody owns, watch them

jump off, run up four flights of an east village walkup
to smell the urine in the hallway
see the claw-footed tub in the kitchen, hear a baby crying,
keep listening past a standing room crowds' applause
and you'll hear a voice banging against the wall
see a guy going thru their bags for money
their dedicated kids forced off the page
into clinics & welfare lines by mothers
who'll do whatever it takes,
always in mourning: it's one man or another
shrouding the truth…If you still
don't believe what you see in their voices
feel the cold bars of a night's lockup
in every word they read, and when it's over
the years abridged to a half hour
punk girls grown plump middle aged
looking like somebody's flatbush mother
standing before you, books to sell
surely an optical trick a mistake of lighting
except for the marks on their arms
uncoding in your brain

Stumbling on Jack's Road

Jack be nimble
Jack be quick
Jack jump over
The candlestick.

Jack be nimble Jack be quick
Jack jumped over all the Johns who
couldn't imagine their way past ordinary
walked between lines they never crossed
I'm Jack he said, furious if anyone forgot,
a name which summoned up those who've imprinted
their souls on a nation's myth: the king of the beats
two daredevil SF poets* a president a fighter
at night when his brain speeded so he couldn't sleep
he conjured up the notorious: Jack Legs Diamond
a 16th century pirate called Black Jack…
known as a jack of all trades, he composed, wrote, painted
fast as he could:
    Jack be nimble Jack be quick
    Jack flew into the sky
crashing into middle age, broke
this wasn't supposed to happen, not to a Jack…
he rose up out of a jumble of words
spewed out on paper nobody understood
debt ridden as the country…owed his whole life
to his name that came up empty
a woman needy enough would make him
her child, bring him back to what he was
going to be, back to his namesake
the kind of man I could fall in love with
I'm Jack, he said when we met
only I knew better

The reference is to Jack Micheline and Jack Hirschman

It's the Kid

The kid
takes to his motor scooter
in the unwinding dinner hours,
rides up and down the nerves
of those just crawled out
of subways insect sized
from jobs sweated out, groveling
like his father to afford this place
keep him gap-clothed in private school snobbery;
he's riding his guts hunch into myth
past what he knows with mind
and the life his parents sacrificed
for the death
that kills before death;
on desperado's freedom trail,
he cracks splits their fragile hold
on calm....a woman's furious face
by an open window,
odor of burnt food like gun smoke
chokes the voice out of threats...
sound of lassos hurled
as he roars down the street,
T.V. horses galloping in pursuit
...one final shoot out:
the kid vanishes
into Time Warner history
for the night

For Women: When Then Is Now

four centuries after Abigail Williams screamed witch thoughts
into people's heads, her arms flailing wildly,
uttering strange sounds, a 16 year old girl in Le Roy N.Y.
began doing the same followed by others just as
several people I know got suspicious mammogram findings
and began accusing dead grandmothers they never met.

the devil vanished into the water and soil of
that small upstate village, hid in teenage jealousies

blame pointed toward and away from women
pierced thru centuries to inflict its legal sting;
pricked with pins on warts and pimples
for evidence beyond the spectral or mammography
forced the accused to stand for
hours in a pillory, arms outstretched

like this, a friend showed me
after her needle biopsy; forbidden to move,
sat with her neck twisted one way arms another
as a doctor aimed a needle to the spot,
blamed when he missed, keeps aiming

for the witch inside her—
no one lives outside the circle of blame
I know my turn will come

it is just a matter of time and time is fluid, is the same time
when I close my eyes, when the machine presses down hard
against my collar bone each January and I'm told it must be
                                                    repeated,
I wait for their judgment
for a harsh winter to turn benign

It's a Road That Goes Straight Ahead in a Circle Straight Ahead

too many men feeling me up these days
rough clumsy hands all over
my breasts pelvis in my cunt
I lie still pretend it's ok to be jabbed like this
doesn't hurt sometimes
as once a girl
wondering if something was wrong
before I heard a braille I understood
and my body answered for me was me
now like in my youth
except I call the men doctors
and when I get their permission
   get dressed
   I'll be waiting outside
I'm back in hot Mexico City
with my first man
only then when **it** was over the **it**
it was all about
he got up relieved dressed
and I lay waiting

The Thing About Blame

Sometimes the day is a sidewalk
I'm walking down like that perfect fall morning

I could have turned back when a crash struck
walked away from the crowd
rushing toward   before that car
turned the wrong way around
revealed its twisted fender
if the day had let me
                    not seen
the other car, people in and out of it crying
a woman on a stretcher
her bloody bandaged head, EMS workers
placing an oxygen mask on her

someone saying she was on the sidewalk
when it happened later wasn't certain

sometimes the day won't let me get off
takes an abrupt turn
and throws me to the ground

———————

a nine-and-a-half-year-old child is sitting up
in the middle of the street calling for help;
she is wearing a chartreuse colored dress
with tiny dots or triangles on it…

it was June
the child ran out between cars without looking

the driver didn't see her   they said it was her fault

September now
the woman might have been on the sidewalk

when she was struck, no one could tell me for sure

the girl lied, said Josephine called her
the woman didn't say anything:

blame bloodied the street
splintered like the bones in the girl's leg
an iron rod held in place what in time has melded:
a scar gives no definite clues…

there's a woman I never met
a girl struck by a car decades ago
crying out to me
a day that's a sidewalk I'm walking down

Lost in a Comic Trying to Be a Graphic Novel

I'm driving thru familiar looking streets
boarded up newsstands, grocery stores
ballooned into gourmet markets
hard to find anything except
sushi and protein energy bars
pass tenements like the one
I grew up in, hated, now couldn't afford
to live in, one family homes gentrified
rooming houses I've moved in & out of
the same, block after block, veering off
I head into a different time zone,
a working class neighborhood
with rents upgraded by new English names
like Kensington, Windsor Terrace
otherwise looks the same except
no one is standing on corners
smoking or drinking from bagged cans of beer
shouting wisecracks after women, but
boom boxes shrunk to notebook size
are still wired to those same heads—
keep turning corners, crossing
street after street to check out
a new apartment new job without ever
leaving this car, though it's funny, because
I never learned how to drive…
sweltering heat on one block
a snow storm on another, pass through
so many time-weather zones
imagine I must be getting older…
when I was ten a car like this one
flung me into the air—
I crashed down splintering a bone in my leg
in a dancer's dream on one of these streets
this car is abruptly lifted up
as in an action comic

only the superhero is missing
and in this car I can't get out of
never learned to drive keeps circling
the same area searching for a runway

Two Photos

1.
A Stand in for Zelda

It's 1920's art deco and isn't life just perfect
music breaks the photographic barrier
flappers are doing the Charleston
money is plentiful and this confident looking
woman my friends admire
wearing t-strap satin shoes seated on a porch
standing on a rooftop in a long beaded dress

looking so confident in a black fur-trimmed coat leaning
against a glass door whose geometric shapes match
her tri-cornered hat, this woman owns the world.
Yes, my mother, I say proudly

killing another woman with those words.
I never wanted to be like her,
to fade into a house dressed marriage of survival,
a woman who pinched love out of pennies to feed us
more than food I ate without knowing
or what my ballet classes cost her…

she smiles at the daughter she hasn't yet conceived;
I smile back reaching across decades
to the woman who raised this poet.
To begin renegotiating old boundaries

2.
A Transitory Moment

I call him father, proud of
that handsome European-looking man
in the sepia photo next to hers,
but no more father to me
than husband to her....

his thick auburn hair brushed back
tints the air, warm like sun, something
that would feel good to nestle in;

I can see where you got your kindness from
or was it compassion my friend said
and does it matter which since
both weren't what he had left to give.

In his face, the wide open innocence of
new country greets me:
America about to be discovered
America in the mind and yearnings before
he ever conceived of that other country he'd spend
a lifetime struggling to survive in, his first born
a daughter he never conceived of,
a wife swept into the hardscrabble thirties
so fast, he didn't recognize her;

I wish I could have been that man's child,
their daughter, grew up in that country
he journeyed to without ever arriving
we now look out on together

For the Promised Elixir of Immortal Health a Friend Tells Me To

think blue: think antioxidant: every berry shade you can eat, drink
blue purpling to grape to cranberry, sky blue sipped
from a straw nobody sees as you lie naked on the beach
seeps into your pores thru the sun's deadly rays
let blue play with your head as you sleep dreaming
thru Egypt's magical blue waters,
feel boysenberry sounds on your tongue
as you wake, preparing the ritual blue meal;

If I told her my birthstone is sapphire
the blue stone that defines my life
an amulet and curse
would it convince her I don't need her instructions
I who've ridden Coltrane's blue train to the end of the line
slid down so many twelve-bar-blues I've lost count
who can't swim and fear water
swam up from immeasurable depths,
breathing morning glory days for months
wrapped in the arms of another
till out of the blue, gone / my heart stopped;
nobody called out code blue
but if they knew
as I walked among them, if they knew....

Giving Thanks

November, 2012

It's cold on top of cold that never cracks
cold that lies in wait on this unlikely November warmth
one day after Thanksgiving

and I am so thankful for it for being able to live
in denial, to push back the cold of other people's mortality
for one more day, to over indulge in the selfish fantasy that
what happened to those friends has nothing to do with me
thankful for feeling like an adolescent whose future is open ended
planning for a time beyond some projected death date
statistics determine for every generation
                                              most of all
I am thankful for being left untouched in this storm-ravaged city
and knowing that I have been lucky this time
to stop there, savor it like a whipped cream topped deep rich
the richest piece of chocolate cake the kind
they say isn't good for you

The Inevitability of What's Random Or

It's just a word

I keep slipping on struggle to keep my balance
and fall off   the word flies up
teasing me as I try to grab hold of it
while clinging to a man's words,
we were meant to be and another's to his wife
that all the poems he wrote before he met her
made her come true* except that word

is like one of those floaters in my eye
morphing into a stray bullet flying thru a window
to kill a sleeping child
a car veering off the street onto a sidewalk
striking a woman exiting a store
                         just random
what newscasters said of several meteors
sighted recently; I let go of his
meant to be when the doctor says my poor bone density
is hereditary, but... I say
only there was no but for my mother
I glimpse being wheeled across the word after
her hip fracture or me now

stuck between random and inevitable
certain there are no accidents, and knowing there are

---

from "The Impossible Indispensability of the Ars Poetica" by Hayden Carruth

An Old Wive's Tale or a Rip Van Winkle Story

Step on a line, break your mother's spine
Step on a hole, break your mother's sugar bowl
Step on a nail, you'll put your dad in jail

"Step on a crack, you'll break your mother's back"
nothing about stepping over it, landing on the other side
stooped over in pain, the weight of seven decades presses down on you;
"step on a line, you'll break your mother's spine"
she's long dead it's your spine, came down
a curved genetic road to find you
after your father left, the man of the house;

cracks formed, the fine line between decisions
stepped over without consequences widened as
you walked the same pedestrian route habit mapped:
easiest distance between years: from home to work to the
same restaurant you and your mother once frequented

a struggle now to stand upright, you fight against
the downward gravitational pull of seventy years;
I do what I can, errands, simple tasks; not enough
the doctor gives you shots; it takes away the pain

you go back to who you were
and can never be again…

who's that old woman in the picture, my mother once asked
when I showed her a photo I took of her one day…
who's that man hunched over a cane I once couldn't
keep up with he walked so fast, who's that angry man
raging against injustice who reminds me of my father
….what happened to the one I've been leaning on all these years?

Long Hot Summer

Words that once rumbled through city streets
sent seismic quakes thru us
drove my mother's fears: the threat of polio
dangers outside the home
kept me from camp, the beach, doing
whatever made the heart beat faster,
erupted in my father's two week vacation
I'd spent all year dreading;
anger heating up our three room apartment
had me running outside into hottest summer since …
for relief…those long hot summers

of Brooklyn boardwalks I lay beneath,
my young girl's face scratched by a boy's beard,
marks I'd both hide and wear like badges in the
ambivalence of new womanhood

words that now leave me comatose:
I move in slow motion thru a thick wetness
in this 10th year of a new century.
Terrible things are happening elsewhere;
my mind registers them. The news registers the temperature.
Someone once called me a survivor,
meant as a compliment, I think,
but roaches and ants survive.
When did surviving mean anything more than
slipping over an edge as if it wasn't there

October's Trick

a month that colors its dead to look so alive
is not a month to be trusted and yet

just yesterday I longed to be in New England when it peaked
go hiking in the woods as I once did with a man I called husband
but I am not that person anymore and he's long gone

I get what color I can now from these Brooklyn trees:
days pumpkin in my face preparing for Halloween
orange like the sun like happy and
I'm trying to be
thankful for another man's long friendship

to be generous enough in this time of aching joints
to accept her in his life whose youth returns
the youth of his imagination:

to let October give him what I can't

My Name Rings in the New Year

a slight barely noticeable and less even than
my brushing it off like a fly from my cheek
when my turn came and someone
called out my name—
I stepped inside it, reaching in
to every single letter till my name fit
like my own skin, faced the audience
and showed them: my name is what wasn't said
is the poem I am breathing thru, it's what you see
and what you don't; my name is my voice
the ghost of a woman's soul
my name is this new year's resolution
made and carried out before
I could break it, having just done what
I swore I would never do, and didn't
just happen; my name is mystery

Going Somewhere Who's Going Somewhere

there & not there on
Astor place with Nina   Saturday July night
leaning against K-Mart absurdity:
crossroads of a world where
out of place has place
people swarming with packages
anything to hold into twilight/dark...

there & not there as
a man packs up his wares
another spreads his out
from everywhere come to
set up shop in our heads...

    must be a party someplace
                          Nina says
not budging from K-Mart window/
jazz taped live from one of the
tables burning incense thru
car exhaust spreads grass fumes
stales *cool* and
doesn't quite give that kick
it once did...

buying or is it selling eyes
question over me but
no sniper with
a firecracker in his fleshed soul
to send this crossroads
roaring into the sky again

    good band at birdland
                        Nina says

means a subway to midtown
and nobody's
going anywhere tonight
on Astor place

September Poem

I am September's child, month that birthed me
and fled three days later; the weeks are
like a wish I'm traveling on toward that day
month that cannot decide
which season it is, the 7th month
on the Roman calendar, god's number
month of the great fire of London
of the Second World War and
the attack on the world trade center
day the 11th became the whole month
and wasn't just that one day I lay
crouched in a fetal position waiting
to be let out…this year

the weather was beautiful like a painting all week
I didn't know what I was doing in it or why those
three women were walking down the street toward me
each with an infant in a pouch around their breasts
or how I became the fourth woman
the years didn't add up to the right number for it
and didn't make any sense but I am
September's child and they never did
even when they should have—

I blow out the days like candles:
make a wish a voice says
which one I ask

II—The Missing Key: U

Yes, the Ducks Were Real

Maybe it was the ducks
with their iridescent heads
so fierce looking reminded me
of the menacing sea gull
on the cover of *Provincetown* poems
place the poet disliked
as I dislike it here, in
lower Manhattan

almost didn't look real
like their orange feet bright yellow beaks
were painted...fearless
one swooped up from the pond
dove right into the Hudson
barely skimming heads of startled onlookers

first hot Sunday of the year...
people unclothed athletic
biked, skated, furiously ran
to keep death at bay a little longer
collapsed on the grass
last summer's West Nile mosquito threat
forgotten in this year's new
stock plunging fears

...or maybe it was the soprano sax
guy was playing on the next bench
like it continued from jazz I heard
in my lover's arms
one Brooklyn night
on the East River promenade

needed to hear it now
be as we were
after the poet introduced us

before the sobriety
I begged him for
reasoned out the passion…

Poet went every fall
to Provincetown because
his wife liked the light
to paint what it allowed her to see,
did it for her;
in those early morning hours
she slept

he dredged up out of season
local fisherman's struggle to survive
catch enough to feed his family…
veering off crowded jazz heated streets
where the burnt-out come yearly for escape
from what pays for this,
brought up what was sunk, drowned
accidentally caught in nets
and so what
desperation hunger making men less…killers almost

…the poet found death
and laid it out on the page,
is trying to tell me something
I don't want to hear…

I haul up my own dead
to discard it: those last
misunderstood years between us
my too late humility…

To come to the poet
in his great neediness,

what would it have cost me...
And what does my pride matter now?

...He needed to force death out into the open
face it like a man
before it soon got him
in a sneak attack one night,
only way he could win
in a no-win;

I've never been to Provincetown
have no desire to go...
but today, forgive me

I need a damned good lie
something prettied up
to dig out my own truth

get back what
can't be given back
in this life

The Missing Key: U

I noticed the letter U missing from words I typed
and needed to press harder on that key
but sometimes I'd forget, fifteen minutes would pass before
I realized you weren't here, and
went back to correct

silly misunderstandings we had like after that party
when you drank too much and
I threw a vase across the room
you threw a plant
pieces scattered over too many years
to glue back with sorry...
I was too the night I fell into Robert's eyes
and needed to be rescued

I must press thru
the fine print of weekly trivia, of credit statements
and job worries, demands of friends & a cat to rescue you
search thru all the places you should be
words that don't make sense
without you...

when I came down with pneumonia
and 103 I heard you say,
"it was like sleeping beside a radiator;"
I don't question, why those words, not others
or how a bout of flu and pneumonia
burning at the same intensity 15 years apart
brought U back. Like I don't question why
it feels so good to be alive.

Crossing Lines

there's a line I keep crossing without getting anywhere
like that stretch of tracks that abruptly begin and end
I stumbled on crossing Fort Hamilton Parkway one day—
there were state lines I crossed
to be with a married man who crossed America
several times trying to leave home

a street I wasn't allowed
to cross as a child,
but did anyway to visit a friend
in one of those tree lined big house blocks
I'd pretend was mine till I heard
doors slam angry words, a woman crying
and no longer believed
I'd ever crossed over to anything

Summer Solstice

The day we met—longest day, someone said;
I didn't know then that

a day that could stretch across years
could be used like that blanket I nestled into
for human warmth as a child,
day its sun would never set, path thru every kind of darkness
a mother's death, those friends… before goodbyes were said,
day I'd take comfort in with him long after
his ashes filled an urn,

longest day he said, day the towers were attacked
blocks from our home, and stranded in Brooklyn
without him, slept on a friend's floor;
day I'd live inside like the wedding ring
he couldn't afford to give me

and no amount of gentrification could change
the area around St. Marks, that corner
where we stood, trying to decide and then
…what the hell…

day when I feel unattractive, unloved
like a magic potion returns my youth
with its myriad possibilities—
a day that never ends in night

Whenever and Always

crossing the space outside the Brooklyn courthouse
I saw a bird struggling to pick up a whole piece of bread
a man carrying a suitcase walking toward the bird
      stoop down and heard him say,
         "Take a small bite. You'll never get the whole piece"

triggering another man's voice in my head:
      "We only had moments, that's all there ever is,
         just moments," he rubbed into a wound
I didn't know was there and wasn't then
my silence mistaken for something else;

I walked past the man still trying
to talk reason to the bird, the other moment

long passed a way for me to tell him,
whenever I pull out a piece of our time
it's like pulling out a thread; the whole fabric of
our life together unravels

Unfinished

> *"Flight delays as JFK airport runway (is) taken over by turtles!"*
> The Daily News, 6/29/2011

this is about dozens of turtles
a mid eastern restaurant we sat in on Atlantic Avenue
                                    hungry and broke
turtles crawling onto the tarmac at JFK
delaying flights for over an hour
this is about watching you slowly bite off
a piece of lamb from a skewer as
you watched me do the same and we
inched our way thru couscous into baklava
                                    past closing time
turtles crawling toward the grassy marshlands
on the other side of the runway to lay their eggs
this is about me wondering what it feels like
                                    to be a turtle…
we never looked at the bill
we kept eating the waiters kept looking at their watches
air traffic controllers threw up their hands in frustration
people sat in planes waiting for the turtles to get across
nobody asked what they do once their eggs were laid
                                  where they'll go

this is about love sick turtles
It is about a meal we never finished

An Apple Isn't a Peach

If I throw it into a poem
It becomes the forbidden fruit and
the whole damn Adam & Eve business
obliterates us with its mythic chatter
I want to spit it out with the skin
and a lot of bad memories that follow
red greens sours everything I want to keep
the day I watched you bite into a peach
caught your desire in my mouth
before asking *do I dare* bit down into
the fleshy pulp right down to the core
both of us lost in that day
a peach became a golden apple

Two Words

he could jump a fence, shoot up walls
back in the Dominican Republic,
a skinny nothing much of a body kid
nobody expected anything from or
here in Bed-Stuy where he
leapt up two steps at a time to the roof
almost ducking the knife that marked his left cheek
I saw in his *tell me about yourself* first day
college English essay

watched him grab and shop lift for the last time
making a fast getaway, jumped high as he could
to land here, staring at the first wall
he couldn't leap over, each word
a brick, fourteen rows, not a single chink
to get a foothold beginning
"When in disgrace with fortune and men's eyes"*
well, he knew about fortune nobody he knew had any
stared at it the way my cat stares at
a tall bookcase takes a few steps back
then forward gauging the distance needed to make the leap
"Desiring this man's art, and that man's scope"
I could see him pacing his mind, considering
the words from different places
"deaf heaven" brought up his mother's
shawled head bowed in prayer every god damn day
when, I don't know how, happened so fast
he was up and over that wall: *life sucks,* he yelled out
holding up a photo of a woman on his cell phone
the couplet he'd snatched hold of
as he once grabbed something from an open market
and ran with it: "For they sweet love rememb'red such
wealth brings
      That then I scorn to change my state with kings."

All quotes are from Shakespeare's sonnet "When, in Disgrace with Fortune and Men's Eyes"

Halloween, 2008

I'm told to prepare for the worst:
a 50-50 chance your namesake
won't make it
flips the day on its wrong side:
the dead are supposed to return
not snatch the living from us
I snap at you; it's a month before
the anniversary of your death…

for two nights he lies in caged fear
force fed, hooked up to I.V.s
balancing between two worlds…
once home soft cries mark his territory:
this rug, that corner, my chair
too weak to jump on my lap, a table
he slumps down humiliated.
I prepare for the worst;

that night, as if someone flung him at me
from a great distance, I wake up
to feel him rubbing against me—

eating from his bowl
shedding his ghostly spirit
through the house,
back as if he never left,
and you, who'd never been here,
most certainly haven't

Snowlight

I didn't know snow could feel so hot
or how much I craved the brightness,
that snow could act like sun if
that's what the eye needs, until
that morning after weeks of grey
I woke up to snow piled against
my window its brightness lit up
the inside of everything
I wanted to throw off the covers
fling open the window and let
the 30 degree snowlight warm me
as once, nestled in my lover's arms
I felt it, the same, exactly *like sun* I told him
you feel like sun

In the Terrible Final Months of 2012

down December streets narrowed by trees
an evergreen lie forces on this grey, rainy day
taped sleigh bells blare Santas out of songs trying
to rewind the year back and get stuck in
                I'm dreaming of...
pictures my mother tore out of a book before
I could color the forbidden into her Jewish daughter's life
a lover would years later do a child's why gets

mixed up in a woman's in a wintery swirl of
fake snow cries for peace mouthing *why* merry and
why yearning back to the night before
a full moon tugged at the earth, the jet stream
changed a loud pop or crack of thunder
awakens my mother gone ten years: a woman
busy tearing up death in a coloring book

Off the Record

I don't like running into you
suspect you feel the same:
those brief job-talk-minutes
barely conceal the mourning garb
we have no right to wear & wouldn't…

        outlaw widows
we grieve for our Marlboro / poet men
same as any black widowed ancestor…
what jumps your words

    shouldn't have happened
    he stopped smoking years ago

and mine

    it was the liquor I minded
    not the packs of pall mall
    smoked out his manhood
      2ND JOY breathed in
    I couldn't get enough…

tough survivors
we both knew the danger

but not everyone who survives
goes on living…

42nd Street on a Saturday Night

Corralled off sidewalks onto streets
beneath the technological fallout of flashing billboards
everyone is breaking down digital...

the man I am with has vanished into his watch
his eyes force down the watch hands
it is 7:45, we have fifteen minutes to get there
what is wrong with me he says without speaking

the crowd thickens, feels like dust
blowing in my face, and how we move
isn't like walking feels like riding on horses,
I tell him this without speaking, riding slow so slow
he looks at me as if I'm crazy

a slow motion stampede of people
riding thru every color of sound
thru the flash of gunshot speeding lights,

do you hear it do you see
we've been flung back in time
I tell him with my eyes body turning
up down everywhere but

he is too far into his watch to hear me....
It is one minute to eight; a huge billboard
drops down before us
we are standing in front of a theater

that may or may not be real
like the man who just stepped out of his watch

Ex Wives Caught in the Jam

it felt as if he had thrown the jam right at her
when he returned to their table
where they usually sat
saw the measly amount in the cup
heard her say she noticed it immediately
and didn't say anything to the waiter, he roared
heads turning their way saw him
fling his two ex wives at her who
would have spoken up for him
telling her exactly when both had
…she didn't remember what else was said
as they left the restaurant and he became nice again
but knew that no matter how hard she tried
she'd never entirely wash off all the jam from her face

The Starting Gate

It's that moment just
before the horses break out
not the race itself or the bets placed
but that moment I thought of
one Brooklyn morning on an F train
as it pulled into my station
everyone turned toward the doors
as if anticipating a subway messiah
the train stops but the doors
don't open not right away
every morning the waiting time
lengthens and
just like at the track when
the horses burst out
a gasp let loose envelopes us

so that morning on the verge of
packing up my life once again
it wasn't a new place new city another job
I was fixated on but
the starting gate
those train doors
waiting for them to open

Call Him Pegasus

aka Barbarus

sweaty men in work clothes
busy harnessing animals to myth
didn't see a winged horse
about to fly off earth

too long since Merlin ruled a county
and first moon-walks
since I flew on something more
than a plane—
I'd never followed the races
         but that day
jumped on same as everyone...

ghosts jockeyed for position
it's a wonder the living man wasn't toppled...

so that day there was him and all the rest
as long ago in a tiny bedroom
looked like a cathedral my first lover said
room packed with ghosts
where two kids tried and failed
to have for just ourselves
as afterwards I'd tried and failed with others....

death is a wound a broken leg
what must heal with time...
vets who knew better said
there's a chance during half a dozen surgeries
and the nine months birthing time
he clung to life...you see
it wasn't just the horse we needed to be all right...

and wasn't just a horse
euthanized

III—Matisse Poems

Almost Naked

Decorative Figure on an Ornamental Background 1925

In the room where Matisse keeps her
a geometry of shapes bloom lush patterns
rugs so thick it would be easy to sink into
lose herself in what colors her space
believe it is the gravity that keeps her
from falling into zero. Naked except
for a white towel wrapped around her thigh
she stares straight ahead as if she were somewhere else.

My mother who preferred serene nature scenes
to paintings like this…like what I would ask if she were here,
could make anything with a needle using thread or wool,
never followed a pattern, organized her days around chores,
evenings around a husband's complaints, lived inside
the gold ring of marriage…afterwards

when he was gone and she was in the home
she'd go thru the motions with her hands
pulling invisible thread through a tiny needle's eye
threading one free breath after another;

it's not so much the woman as the patterns
I'm drawn to, how she fits in and doesn't
whether she's toying with his vision
or he led her to it

Matisse's Version Versus Mine

Odalisque in Red Trousers, 1924 -25

I know how she feels, lying there
looking so content, how much effort it took
to watch him admire his work,
satisfied that he's finally got her
to let him believe it—

In the days when I only wanted to please a man
I recall lying like that for hours beside someone
who slept half the day so as not to wake him

her limp body tells one story,
her black eyes another…how could he not
have seen what he gave her

felt the veins in my neck tighten
when he put his arm around me as someone
approached him that day in the West End bar

I didn't throw it off as I would have
if some slimy thing had dropped down on me
a dirty dish rag fallen from a shelf
I did nothing…. a white brush stroke
on negative space, black scrawling bar noise
tangled around three people…

I haven't thought of that man in years, those nights
I lay dead beside him, what happened that didn't happen
but it's all there…just as thru digital imaging I can now see how
Matisse struggled scraped, and rescraped his canvas with
a nerve edged knife, see the original outlines of his vision
what it took for him to get there

for me to view it in exactly this way

Nobody & Nothing

Matisse, Moroccan Landscape (Acanthus) 1912

What a relief!
to lose myself in this bluegreen this
fertile unspoiled mind for the
time it will take me
to write this poem, in those few
second minute moments
I have wiped out every nagging ghost,
on this day, my birthday
there will be no reparations made to the dead;
turned upside down, earth becomes sky
jungled with lush green
clouds waterfall in the distance;
how easy it is to believe in such a day
till something…looks like a creature of some sort
leaps out from behind a tree—
before his black eye nails me
I break out of this poem…

Listening to *The Trapeze Performers* by Matisse

the sound of his color
is the sound of jazz is the sound of
yellow breaking thru lawn green
shattering this day full of terror plots
is purple rage breaking up thru every color of
injustice overriding bullies who
kill with words with cameras
is the blues dancing off the edge my cry
louder louder when I hear the
impact of his scorching orange
on all teetotalers when I don't want to
cover my ears to shut out the noise
louder louder against those who
water down life with fear
when the loudest sound becomes the
sound of color improvising breath

The Caption Reads: *Madame Matisse with Manila Shawl*

I.

I don't care what he called her, when
I saw the woman in that embroidered shawl
like she wore, I knew; wasn't that arrogant pose either,
took Matisse to bring it out in her
it's all in the eyes, what they see, as in those daguerreotypes
she collected, one face mirrored beneath another

and it's in the word stroke, too—
a stroke of luck to find a mentor
morphed into a second mother, I thought, before I knew
how that would stroke conflicting needs, escalate
after the piano I gave her
to get rid of what someone left behind,
more than two decades before,
the paralyzing stroke:

kept hitting the keys
and nothing not a single sound, she said...
been a year now, and nothing, they said

II.

adopt me I joked the day she and her husband discussed options
after the miscarriage; *hear that she said to him.*
I'd baby sit, the older sister
stepchild, annoyingly helpful, always underfoot
she couldn't let go; or I who
house sat while they vacationed, place a friend called
the ass end of Brooklyn, escaped my hot
one room studio-life, forgot who and where I was

ventured out one day by accident, a little more, then
further, still with that invisible leash

afraid to pull off or she yank free of…

no sound. nothing.
rippled beneath two whole decades
and then some…quarrels don't always
speak out loud

III.

I grew into my own life, rarely thought of her
except now and then out of curiosity,
checked on-line to see what she was up to,
a thought of someday showing her how far I'd come
in part because of her
in greater part because I got away
wiped out now in one felled stroke…

maybe isn't even she, anymore
than that woman Matisse painted.

The Family

The Painter's Family, 1911

two boys in identical red outfits are playing chess
in a family room; a woman seated on a coach doing...
I don't know what with her hands, perhaps embroidery;
my mother always crocheted, silent like her
two long needles turning my father's angry rant
into white spread cover-ups...

a looming black presence stands apart
forcing herself into my field of vision;
no one in this room is speaking but
I can hear them

in the clashing patterns of
the oriental rug, the two coaches,
in the scatter rug and wall paper,
in the red-dotted tile fireplace

I could hear it then, too...
my father's anger bounced off my brother
who'd sit there intent on his homework
like those two boys silently playing chess,
his other self hidden...if he had a color
it would be something neutral, like beige

then the woman in black,
then me...
I like color, bright, on the edge of flashy
I wore my black inside then,
what matters is not the color so much as her position
in relation to the others, patterns
Matisse can't extricate his family from

where I was then and am now

IV—To Those Looking Down...

To Those Looking Down: Watch, Listen

Rat, I thought, seeing that dead animal,
could have been a small squirrel or large mouse
by the cellar steps where I put out food the night before
for two black cats I feed, but
kept coming back to rat

                 flung it out loud at
a white-shirted tie-flung-over-his shoulder guy
ahead of me rushing thru the heavy metal subway turnstile
his hand flying back against it, smacked me in the face
blood squirted from my nose; people offered tissues
he tossed out *sorry* like a black rose,
I'm in a hurry vanishing down the steps...

the rat outside my building was still there next morning.
I walked around it, picked up the cats' plates
put them on the other side and quickly ran in
to wash my hands...first one rat then
hundreds, soon a whole town infected dying,
recalling Camus' *The Plague*

all you really need is one rat....
saw homeless fear in a former colleague's eyes
a decades old best friend of his boss, a man trying to
show higher ups he's keeping costs down,
get a promotion, told him, *you're no longer needed...*
over 50 is no longer needed

I kept hoping the rat would be gone each morning
that a neighbor or the part time super
would get rid of it...

I've never been good at getting rid of rats
once at a job, in my bed, my home

put up with it longer than I should have
than anyone ever should…

the fourth morning the rat was gone from my building;
even if it was a small squirrel, as my neighbor thought,
I saw a rat…others were seen

on the terrace of the Cipriani club at 55 Water Street
looking down at the crowd protesting thousands of firings
looking down at scared, hungry, out of work
for months, a year or more, others
drinking champagne and looking down

a crowd armed with mental pesticides gathered around Wall Street
quickly grew ignoring boundaries, spread
across economic lines, across bridges and state lines;
In less than a week they outnumbered the 1%
                                          looking down

A Terrible Beauty*

There was no mistaking the similarity
between his cypresses or sunflowers and
what I saw in that first photo flaming up from the ocean
that same thickly layered intensity;
I thought of the artist who
could have painted it, what madness
drove his mind, what madness to have
let what I looked at in awe happen…
death still unseen washing up
on the shores of that photo
while I, struck by something so
utterly beautiful and terrible

as if it had nothing to do with that
sea bird I later saw dripping with oil
whose one visible eye filled with
such depthless sadness, as he sat immobilized
looking out helplessly at me from my computer.

What took my breath away
lingered independently of it
like smoke from a cigarette that brings back
the familiar warmth and excitement of first times…
same cigarette that kills.
And it doesn't matter. As soon as
someone lights up…

Do you smoke, they kept asking me in the hospital.
No I said. Not now. When?
If I'd said when everything was then
would they have understood anymore than
I can, who could see an explosion of beauty and art
in what destroys it…chokes the life out
of what's alive

"A terrible beauty is born" is taken from the poem, "Easter 1916" by Yeats

Those Poems Like Safe Houses

With apologies to the outlaw poets

caught up in the rush of fast flying bullet words
sending Billy the Kid & Dillinger on
bank robbery sprees the kicked up
dust from a horse or the screech of cars
burning rubber in a fast getaway
and the pure 21st century joy of watching
banks that robbed us held up until
                       that hot June midnight

death spilled out of words blood mingled screams
from a Colorado theater blew across America
it wasn't only banks robbed now
or then either we like to forget
boundaries blurred no one knew if it
was happening on screen or off
                       until they did...

a night to remember people said just before,
clinging to their tickets to Batman's cape to
be lifted up out of their everyday to fight a bad guy
only he never had a chance
someone yelled, *does anyone know how
to shut that movie off* shut off a maniac's mind
shut off our fascination with outlaws
without killing the outlaw spirit

Stand Down

I'm tearing up lettuce cutting up cucumbers tomatoes
not thinking about the upcoming week's problems
turn the T.V. volume down on some sports event till 60 minutes
begins: its news story *Stand Down* shoots the volume up

out of my control into another tense
a truce between the past and present is broken

I watch vets crowd around tents asking for help: treatment jobs
and it's 1993 again…we are at the first stand down
a vet salutes him and he salutes back salutes a future intuited

I do not travel beyond that day an outsider
I am taking it all in happy just to be together

the news commentator focuses on some homeless vets
he was never homeless not physically but was
mentally he told me years later trying to make me understand
what it's like to become voiceless:
"can hear the tune cant sing"*

I couldn't stop and he didn't want me to
but there it was impassible

stand down: at ease a temporary ceasefire
a Walt Disney survival fantasy:
word like a rock someone on a cliff throws off
hitting a person in a passing car

---

* From "the boys in the band" by Andrew Gettler

A Roach Poem

It's the ones found in New York walkup apartments
I grew up in, century old brownstones I've lived in
and sometimes like now been lucky for years
                                              then

in a space 52" long, a half inch wide
too small for the eye to crawl thru but
big enough for imagination to run with
between the stove and sink counter my luck ran out;
I plunged a knife down to see just what / how far
                                                and then
the killing began; for every one I got
smaller ones appeared; determined
I unleashed an arsenal of insecticide whose fumes
sent me flying down a familiar Nam vet's voice
into another country sent me to a tunnel near Saigon

so small it was hard for him & his men to get thru
see what booby traps were set where whole
villagers, factories, bomb shelters existed and
clearly now sent me out of my rational mind…
small Vietnamese soldiers morphed into hundreds of
roaches digging this tunnel in my kitchen for years
traps set for them trapped me in a killing mindset:
I didn't just want to eradicate them from my apartment
but to take out an entire species…
it's a losing battle I heard him say and vanish
an exterminator came, sprayed, plugged up holes
be back he said on his way out, leaving his bill
and a pronoun I couldn't catch

Shoveling

1.
they clutch huge shovels walking down
I'd say my block but it is theirs,
men who decades ago moved into this country
not its language, staked down their Italian souls
overwriting deeds to their property
with herbs enormous sunflowers
every variety of bloom
...no space left they keep planting

people pass admiring...*can I have...*
a smile a nod gives permission
to pull up a bunch of thyme or rosemary
this garden that corners Court & Carroll Streets
                              Brooklyn
outside their clubroom this block over which
the bandiera d'Italia flies freely from rooftops
what's left of their neighborhood before
I and those like me came
2.
they walk three abreast small dark clothed
fluttering of wives seen now & then...
only one nods, tips his hat slightly when I pass...
the men keep walking determined

the snow keeps falling
layers of ice coat the tops of hedges
the walkways men's souls;
Egypt floats off peoples' tongues as they pass
the men look at each other understand
what lies outside language

what my Russian born father would have
understood why they crack down so hard
on the ice fly the old countries' flag from their homes

keep shoveling securing what's theirs
by deed by work by what cannot be tallied,
men who live in the language of each others countries
        Italy   Russia   Egypt
same war fought same victory to be won

The Storm

Oct 28—Nov. 2 2012

the storm didn't stay outside; it entered our streets and yards
uprooted trees smashed through windows and devoured our furniture
the storm still wasn't satisfied

its hunger was insatiable; it frayed nerves and snapped wires
broke into our minds blocking escape routes
thru books and games, stole every kind of light we had

took our breath from us as it poured down our throats
to stop us from talking our way out of it
and flung us away from everything we owned

ripped up memories and played with our minds
unleashed wild animal sounds banging on doors and windows
we took cover with our terrified pets and strangers

and when our mental storm barriers gave we
met in bars cafes and pizza shops to wait it out together
lit up only by flashlights people baked and cooked

prayed to gods we didn't believe in and made
promises about doing better being better
the storm shook the fragile foundations of our existence

we kept on because we didn't know how not to
many were rescued, not all; others will be and
homes and businesses restored or rebuilt;

but nobody will make it back to where we once were

Dire Warnings

we were warned to keep away from strangers
to be suspicious of anyone not like us

people of other races and of different religions from ours
atheists and all free spirits especially artists

we were warned about sleeping in other people's homes
eating food we weren't familiar with

getting overexcited and too emotional about things
of danger lurking in sleep away camp and open road clubs

discouraged from swimming, bike riding getting too much sun
we were warned about touching ourselves and

of men who only wanted one thing
about drugs and sex and how "the more you get the more you want"

we were warned about many things
but nobody warned us about the trees

we played *ring around the rosy* under
that kept the sun from burning us

trees whose leaves dazzled us with color every autumn
infested with fungus or mold and dying of root rot

environmentalists sent out alarms with predictions
we dismissed along with climate change as nonsense

nobody warned us that the trees would become killers
and uproot lifting up slabs of concrete from under us

break thru iron gates into homes flattening cars
killing anyone in their way

nobody warned us…

On Trying to Understand What It Means to Owe Trillions, What a Trillion Even Is

On reading that the national debt tops $14 trillion

I give up; stop searching the internet, dictionaries
and follow what I know in my gut...

it's the cost of an apple, the price of lettuce
I once worried about
that Con Ed bill that goes up with the temperature
the A.C. that breaks and must be fixed or replaced
but cannot keep out the heat

It's a debt that keeps increasing with
warnings of blackouts if the bill isn't paid by a certain date
yeah, I finally get it...it's the process of subtraction,
not of dollars but breaths

nobody knows how many breaths they actually owe—
it's that coach some relative bought on the installment plan
and kept paying for the rest of his life because no one
told him to stop; it's a three room tenement apartment
the landlord coming for the rent...he did every month
                                                   and
it's not exactly that my parents didn't have it,
it's just that they didn't have all of it
that there is no all of it to be had, it isn't something finite
soon, they kept repeating...soon...

a trillion is the highest point I can imagine falling off
a number so large it takes the breath right out of me
but I go on, everyone goes on, we keep on breathing
somebody's dirty air

No Flowers for Terrorists, a Cry for Peace

for those who march against war

All the flowers
flying out of your mouths
are dead,
the air has killed them,
someone has poisoned the air,
all the 1960's flowers,
can't you see them as you march thru the grass,
dead flowers deadly flowers

How much will you sacrifice for peace?

Enough to leave those pretty parks
go by Saint Paul's church and
stare into the dead night of a windowless
building's charred remains

till you see people's flamed wings
spread out as they leapt
and you feel your own skin
burning so bad, you'd kill to stop it,

do you want peace enough

to look at every photo of those missing
since September 11th,
read the rosary of names aloud
as you once read the names of
the South American 'disappeared,'
marched and petitioned us to help
those in Somalia Bosnia, remember,
even went there, some of you,
risked your lives for them…

Almost 3000 dead buried
a few miles from where you live
homes some of you left in fear
afraid to return
breathe air that makes you sick,

toxic excuses…only
the allergies   asthma are real
and the nightmares you wake trembling from,

are you willing to descend into hell
till you cough up all the dead fairy-tale flowers,
your eyes blaze with anger
at what was and isn't
and is, now…
you'll do anything, yes even wage war
to keep this from happening again,

do you want peace enough
to look at a picture of Hitler
and admit that innocent people died then
so you can live now

stop marching long enough
to look around at your city,
imagine one woman taking a plane
one man entering his office,
you'll do anything
to keep them alive
this city you love, safe

how much do you really want peace?

———————

Look at all the flowers,
dead flowers…deadly flowers

It's Because

long before someone filled the word with explosives
and sound reached vocabulary
to echo out of voices across America
I heard it in a mother's *because I said so*
seen it in a boss's eyes, a doctor's set expression
when I asked, *are you sure it's necessary*
picked it up in the unspoken way things are done
in my mother's nursing home
when someone who changed tables at lunch was
ordered back, as if she'd illegally crossed a border
that line that divides order from anarchy
line craved in stone....what stone has anyone ever seen it?
when a seven year old in a Sharon Olds' poem
says to another boy his age,
"we could easily kill a two-year old" at a birthday party
I heard it in an ex-president's *because I can*

why settled in one word laundered thru our lives
                                        why
to stop black markets from financing it
companies tightened restriction on
cigarette marketing in underdeveloped countries
why the PO refused my check without an address
why I must give my Social Security number to use
a xerox machine the college bought for that purpose, why
I asked a professor and got the same response as
from the clerk at the PO, from the pharmacist
who needed to see ID to purchase cold meds
from the bank who said my ID was insufficient
to cash a $25.00 out-of-state check

and though I didn't hear it after the Dec. 26th blizzard
as streets went unplowed, people left stranded
at airports, in stalled trains, cars and in EMS trucks
waiting to be rescued, why a sanitation truck was
parked outside a pizza store, I am still waiting
to hear the mayor explain why weather reports
went ignored, what caused the distraction
                        say
it's because of terrorism

Thumbing a Ride

I'd never hitchiked but standing on a crowded N.Y.C. subway
one morning jammed in so tight I couldn't move,
hundreds of frantic thumbs flashing down virtual roads
wherever I looked, had the urge; to get on that road
before technology paved its gravel dust
smoothed out those hairpin turns, drove it into myth,
to feel every bump as we head west thru
Chicago, Missouri, Kansas to L.A.,
wind biting dust blowing thru the window
and yes, facing unspecified danger from everywhere
but not a road that could be quickly snatched
by someone rushing out a subway door as it opened
throwing me back to a place I never left

The Invasion

think it's just another morning rush hour
on the F train, day before Thanksgiving and
lighter than usual, got a rare seat
not far from a middle aged balding man
muttering something I barely take note of when
I hear warnings about Mexicans
not paying taxes, stealing our jobs,
refusing to learn English, thousands of
Mexicans coming on this train followed by
Dominicans who are no different and
should be sent back where they came from—
doesn't see me or anyone but those immigrants,
hasn't forgotten about the Chinese either
like the Mexicans and Dominicans they
keep entering his country, this subway car,
nobody stopping them, and this poor man,
an American citizen, doesn't he have any rights,
soon he won't be able to read his paper
the Daily News will be written entirely in Spanish,
only one more stop, I can't wait to get off
when the Russians jump on, who've already
taken Coney Island from us, what next
the train pulls into Jay street
and I squeeze out through a crowd of
unruly Mexicans piling on
followed by Dominicans and... and...

Sneaking Across the Border

He never spoke of what it was like
those three years in Amsterdam
waiting to get to America

and I never asked....
I heard about it from her, not him

he & I lived in separate countries;
there was no crossing over, not then;
day after day I read about those thousands
of migrant children....many 17 and younger...

and I hear my mother's voice from
before I was ready to listen, only 17 when his father
forced him to join a group of youths
fleeing Russian pogroms...

In an album she left me are photos of
the family he'd never see again...

using the migrant's story I sneak across the border;
among the children coming thru Mexico,
Central America, some drowning or getting shot

I see that Russian boy
standing with others who made it here
forced to explain WHY what
he'll be asking himself his whole life

What About the Fish?

For long-lost cousin, Allen Stein

"what about the fish," you asked
when they started pumping toxic
water out of New Orleans into the lake—
what about it, I thought
and the 9/11 smoke we breathed in
next generation will cough out;

I knew a man…or my lover did…
whose exposure to agent orange killed
his son born a year after he returned from Viet Nam,
goes on living his death out loud…

"someone will start hollering about it," you said,
                              always does
point the finger of blame, I answered,
take turns at it….remember how it goes
in grade school in the yard,
someone must be **it**…

when the man I loved died
I blamed cigarettes…others,
the environment food / liquor bad doctors
                       when nothing else,
bring back the god we killed last century

The System

we are the ones who jumped without parachutes
into the workplace of America
those out of the system we are in
the part time temporary easily expendable ones
who see the skies past rules break the infinitive
and leap into the unpermitted
those who follow their gut: for that
there's no forgiveness

I think of weeds, the ground cover
providing food and nourishment for the soil
when one flowers like the real thing it is
just weeds they say without looking

I've walked naked thru decades—
look, here in my book   in this magazine
show them what I've done

someone reminds me of a due date
penalties to be paid

Drives thru a Poem Like He's Headed for That Cliff He's Been Over Before

For Hayden Carruth

He's one of those guys who never stops driving,
      eyes always on the road.
When someone is talking, doesn't interrupt either.
Keeps driving, right into the words.
Far in. Even when they stop speaking.
Drives till he's really there.

The weekend Andrew and I were his passengers
he drove thru the backwoods of 70 years;
with his young lady swerved like crazy
thru a funky country, air incensed with
      their erotic love.
Most careful / reckless guy we ever met.
Didn't know it then, but he kept us
from getting into an accident.

She warmed the atmosphere making bread.
Knew we were there for him and moved quietly
      among us.
When they spoke, even something trivial,
they were making love. Never stopped.
Didn't matter what we saw or heard as though
we weren't there sometimes. But he knew.
Amplified our own love. Which needed none.

This was stolen time for him, more than two decades
      on us.
Maybe the pure joy of seeing him with her
      made me forget: us too.
If Andrew had wished, right then on the couch, floor...
      But first, that phone call to make.

Never let on that he saw anything. Just kept talking.

I craned my neck, turning frequently to overhear,
tensed, like someone ready to jump out of a speeding car,
    not thinking of consequences.

He saw where I was headed; slit eyes bore down on me
and he rammed right thru high on the booze
he'd sworn off more than three decades.

Afterwards we drank, talked as though nothing happened.
When Andrew and I were ready, he offered us their bed
    for the night.

V—Without Sound or Sense

Without Sound or Sense

I hate the smell of garbage
rank odors in old hallway buildings
can't stand street drilling, jackhammers
pounding outside my windows
boom box thunder, cell phone voices
buzzing around me like bees I want to swat
voices in knock down drag out fights
kids screaming down the street
a car screeching to a stop inches from
someone's shout, a hey, fuck off
from someone who walks into me while texting
                except when they're absent
and I don't smell any coffee, taste a morning's burnt toast
breathe the scent of freshly mowed grass
of forbidden cigarette smoke or
wake to a helicopter jamming with
a sanitation truck, can't hear
a single subway musician as a train
speeding thru snaps his violin or
guitar strings, when there's no rage or joy
exploding on a street

I can't feel the city's atonal rhythms
in my head, my heart picks up nothing:
thoughts without color or sound swirl around
in weatherless space…the poem is still born

In the Company of Nice People I Keep Quiet

"I don't like nice people," he said
setting off a defense from a young woman who
swore she's nice, thinks most people are;
I kept quiet; he kept looking at me
"most people aren't nice" he said, his eyes
moving from her to me
she gave examples

the ones who over tip in restaurants
ready to help anyone they can
the first to offer sympathy mourn someone's loss
sacrifice themselves
                                           I kept quiet
"even those who appear to be nice," he said
still looking at me still quiet

I am not such a person…
after 9/11 I stood with others applauding
the first respondents when they drove by
to call them nice is to belittle who they are
what they've done…

nice is like an algebraic equation
X plus Y equals every cause
doesn't have a bad word to say about anyone
avoids arguments, agrees with whoever

nice is a uniform, starched buttoned up nakedness
lace-curtain Irish fronting impoverishment
politeness squared: nice is
something I don't want to be called

"What Is the Where?"

title of a Recession Art Show at the Invisible dog art Center

halfway down Smith street
those words stopped me as if I'd come to the corner
and the light had changed, the red of danger, don't go
in a question I couldn't get past
even as I walked past it
down the familiarity of café-lined streets
and stopped to get something to eat
make small talk, still there
as I am still visiting my father in the hospital
telling him I'll be back later, who
shrugged later off like a shroud
as the day I thought of seeing my mother
and didn't her last day
as that missed phone call I'm still waiting
to hear ring thru a new century
to become the where of what
something so abstract I cannot locate it with words
feels more concrete than if I could...

half way down the street thru my life
a young woman who resembles me
whispers in the ear of my soul,
when did you ever wait for a light to change?

Like Any Drunkard

It's the way my cat lifts a paw and
bangs on his bowl as I pick it up
if I don't fill it fast enough
see in his urgency that same
need I once saw in a man
I thought I knew
seated on a stool beside me,
clenching an empty bottle
hitting the bar with it repeatedly
like the bars of a cage
and the waiter busy serving others
maybe didn't hear that
wounded animal whine rise up
each time for if he did would
have done anything to soothe it

It's the Blues

For Tony Moffeit

It's that "spirit language" you hear riding a train whistle
Bourbon Street horns blowing the dead out
of St. Louis cemetery into your thoughts
it's driving on New Mexico's red dust back roads
coyotes in the sagebrush, coyotes howling
in your head, as your car speeds your hand across the page
to New York City sending your blues my way
a hot chili pepper sun sends you ghostly visions: a dead father,
woman still waiting for you in a roadhouse café
you keep looking past at me you can't see
in a crowded subway car, nothing so exotic here as
a rattlesnake woman dancing for whatever I have

it's the same homeless woman by the steps
asking, *any change today, anything at all*
and there's that coyote who won't let you be
that trickster: he's everywhere you look; I saw him today on the news
wearing a suit trying to sell me his opinions, posing as my landlord
saw him behind a desk in the bank, a doctor's office, an insurance office

Indians aren't drumming for rain or the heat to let up here
we pray for the A.C. to keep working, something
to quench our thirst, end the drought in our lives
to make it to our station without being robbed
who've already been robbed of everything

it's that moan of lonesome you hear
crossing state lines coming my way...

On Hearing the James Singleton Quartet

Snug Harbor Jazz Club, New Orleans

dwarfed by his bass this musician
grew smaller as he played with my mind
sound and image pitched above logic—
a trick of the eye saw him
crawl around the bass like a bug
working his way thru chord changes
down strings become frantic
trying to get out getting deeper in
his arms wrapped around its body
watched hands much too small
pull the sun out of a southern night
fleshing hot sweaty sounds
thru this northern soul

Me, Punk and Lou Reed

Punk meant poverty, meant homelessness, welfare
and clinic waiting rooms with crying kids, meant
worn black leather jackets wrapped around shivering
cold Brooklyn tenement and my mismatched parents'
struggling lives caught in the American dream trap—
punk meant Lou Reed back then…

So when news of his death passed from
one person to another past by me
that Sunday, I didn't know what to say.
Said nothing. Winding like a decades long road
sightings of him spotted by one or another
brought him back reeling in song thru the night

and me in search of an old tape flung in
the back of my closet, wiped off the dust
and listened to him get rid of "a life spent
listening to assholes"* searching for his voice
among the hustlers and transvestites in & out
of his 70's underground that

brought back my own in a 4th floor East Village walk up
with a man I went to bed with every night and woke up to
hear my father's voice…don't remember if
it was something I said or didn't say my things
flung all over the apartment, those
half filled cartons of Chinese food spoiling somewhere
and it doesn't matter

or that chorus of voices heard from those
who bore no resemblance to either parent
and years spent trying to "trade in a 14th chance of this
life"*

or that when I choose some music to listen to

it will still be Coltrane or Miles, not him,
it's just that I get it   sex with your parents

no longer sounds ridiculous
or wanting a child past possible

---

*All quotes are from Lou Reed's " Set the Twilight Reeling."

For Iris Berman

the flower you called "untamed...uncultivated" and named for
rooted in the Greek word, rainbow describes your
infinite variety we only saw aspects of
a free-flowing spirit poemed in words and word sounds
bloomed best in the wilds of imagination
wasn't visible to everyone; it took a bit of
trudging through to see what I heard when
you played a poem, your throaty voice,
instrument apart from and part of
"this body" you wrote about

I think of jazz of sounds that go their own way
of the blues, way Van Gogh burst out Iris Joy
on canvas, a perennial flower, Iris

doesn't die in the spring
that's when it blooms.
you, dear friend, should have known better
we do

There's No Stopping It

you've heard them
wrapped in a patched word
aids quilt shaped like California
and covered in worded threads
smelling of hogs with huge holes
a Chicago wind blows through,
or wearing the Statue of Liberty's crown
draped in homeless men & women,
hear them in every state
clinging to their laurel wreaths—
harmless those in power say
assuring themselves it's not a revolution
as slowly they multiply
begin turning up
in every borough county village,
a man on horseback
as far as Montana
flings out a verbal lasso
corralling cowboys
another speaks with the handcuffed voice
of a prisoner rattling in free verse chains
others settle into cafes coffee houses
in towns so small a two block main street
is the town they become—
one regular cat with
a hip hop voice from Queens
reaches for the wreath
someone else grabs
they begin slamming words for it—
news of them reaches
America's anointed one,
wrapped in red white & blue jargon
he's shouting *I have it,*
holding up a crumbling brown wreath
can't you see it, he cries louder

I am the true laureate
      the only one
pitched at too low a frequency,
his words render him invisible

New York Winter, 2012

Something about these mild sunny days doesn't feel right
more like San Francisco not New York
we shouldn't complain only nobody says or says too often
we don't even fight anymore remember last year:
dirty snow that wouldn't melt
people slipping falling into each other
and out the wrong end
things are not exactly green now of course
but like just before day after day
then a hint of blue the icy kind
the doctor calls after a routine exam
asks you to come in there's been a change
someone wakes up beside you angry—
remember last year's ice storm? It's like that
the temperature suddenly drops 20 degrees below calm
we're bundled up in shut down nobody talking
huddled in blankets complaining
there's not enough heat inside and too much
of the other kind   lasts two days
then everything turns mild again
a false alarm nothing to worry about,
he comes home asking how your day was
where you'd like to go for dinner
the 6:00 news points to La Nina's effect
on the jet stream to reassures us why
things are back to the way they're
not supposed to be

With Grateful Acknowledgment to Wallace Stevens

snow thickened the ground outside my bedroom window
      was all I saw of the world that day
the monotonous color of its coldness
not a single animal's footstep marked the small area
      my neighbor's fence blocked off
and worried about what happened to two
      black cats I've been caring for out front
missing now for two days, sat at my desk unable to concentrate
      when I looked out the window and saw
that black bird from Wallace Stevens' poem
      pecking for food in the snow that rose up to him
which like an eye followed me out to where the cats stood
      waiting for me to feed them who'd never really been gone
except in my need for them not to be and
feeling better than I had in a long time
      looked out the window for my bird
who'd vanished and was never mine anymore
      than this poem I borrowed him for
will be once released

Three Exhibits: Inventing Abstraction, 1910—1925

New Photography, 2012
Edvard Munch: The Scream

1.
"I transform myself into the zero of form, I destroyed
the ring of the horizon and escaped from the circle of
things…"—Kazimir Malevich

All I could think about were people starving
as I walked thru this exhibit, some familiar names
others I didn't know and noting

the brush stroke vertical lines of
one artist, geometric shapes of another, didn't really matter;
a woman's face peaked out of the confusion
struggling to free herself, fails and
vanishes in the next artist's colorful swirl
that hit me like a sudden blow on the head…
lines and shapes began to disappear color fade;
I came to the end: everything was white
there was nowhere else to go
but black

2.
It's 1970. A few men are about to be executed.
a life magazine photographer asks the executioners
to hold their fire until he takes his shot, then

turns away, never looks back
several shots ring out but
I only hear his…it is loud, unrelenting

3.
like that scream pitched too high for words
like the sound zero makes
if you could hear it

Young Man with a Guitar

Tuscalousa Alabama 4/29/2011

a young man with a guitar on his back
stares out on piles of rubble...

like photos ripped to shreds, newsprint scatters
this scene across five states pursuing tornadoes

those who survived fled before
the photographer could capture them
who this man will bring back in song
strum guitar strings to resuscitate
those doctors couldn't, rebuild lives

I know this as I know how someone
can be brought back to life line by line in poems
as I know what he must have sacrificed
to have saved his guitar for this purpose

a man who'll never be able to explain
to some woman how he knows
what birth pangs feel like
convince her there's no one else,

this woman he'll meet far from here
who'll sense others breathing down her neck
as he presses close, the smell of
blood clotted earth dust swirling around them

Fear as Loud as a Mugging

to be mugged walking down a street
crowded with people going to & from church
out for brunch or to do some shopping
enjoy this Sunday's relief from the heat
for it to occur so fast the word can't
grab hold of anything as the car speeds off
to feel that my mind has been broken into
and no witnesses to corroborate what
must be happening to others

a mugging that strikes suddenly
like being hit on the head, knocked down
without falling, hip-hopping over my thoughts
forcing me to run out of a store the gym anyplace
run as fast as I can to shake it, as
I once ran from two guys sitting on a stoop I saw
give each other the eye before trying to jump me,
ran like the day I came back jet lagged
from England and didn't see the man in the elevator
follow me down the hall to my apartment
till I felt something sharp sticking in my back
and ran out screaming…

no, nothing was taken
I lie—running from what keeps
slipping out of the word surrounded by people
too deaf to see what they can't hear anymore

On a Flight Hijacked by Diego Rivera

MoMA, Jan. 2012

I can feel him breathing the hot Mexican sun down on me
turning skeletons loose in my head being dragged back
to that Pan Am flight climbing Mexico's dizzying
heights of first love that tequila night a boy broke in
like it was nothing and it was nothing

…I lay in bed afterwards watching him stand by the window
of our hotel ignoring me later dressed in one of
those brightly colored skirts & embroidered blouses
he liked to see me wearing ribbons dangling from my long hair
photographed me till I couldn't stand up any longer

standing here now looking at these murals transfixed by
"The Uprising" watch soldiers bear down
on an angry crowd an enraged woman up front
grabs a soldier's arm his sword flashes across her red dress
like one I might have been wearing

On Diego Rivera

MoMA, Jan. 2012

I am much too small to fit into his imagination
it would overwhelm send
Zapata's horse dragging the agrarian leader off canvas
filter the fields of peasants thru my everyday this & that—

a man so large wouldn't want a woman like me
and I should be grateful...
when an artist like him gets inside a woman
it's one country invading another
one country that survives

Saint in a Sardine Can

a drawing by Donna Kerness

It's how it all gets mixed up in my head
when I look at these drawings

those girls who always smiled apples
for the teacher, starched immaculate white
bloused spilling perfection into notebook pages

mingling now with the smell of sardines—
had to be Norwegian, he said,
sleeping for hours while I lay awake beside him
like some dead thing and the awful smell of sardines
filling every corner of my one room apartment

the same way something snapped when
I was told to change my attitude at work & be like them
I slammed the door so hard as I left, the glass cracked
stacks of papers flew off a desk

flung everything I could find across the room where he slept
waking him out the door out of my life…
never said I was a saint

how lovely they now look in those cans as if
a spell had been cast over them, over me as well
no longer the same dreaded saints of my life
these necklaced in tree twigs, netted in
branched leaf stared gold & silver, lying in some
fairytale forest of new creation, madonnas
with child or not, utterly transformed
by this artist's vision

Who Dares Invoke the Bard?

of the reporter who called Dean's cry, "a mad howl"

What "mad howl"
Allen would have fumed...

a politician's voice speeding
past opponents' leads
thru half a dozen states
ends up whimpering across headlines
next morning
barely breathing
call that a howl...

his ashes stir in his urn
at the very mention...

reminds us who rammed past
Columbia's hollowed gates
more than fifty years ago
freed poetry   a whole decade
the nation marching in lockstep

to breathe in
our own rhythm

the sound that still reverberates

Two Bombs

one bomb went off across the country*
as we sat in Lindy's having dinner on 53rd & 7th,
another at Times Square failed to detonate—

the first of May, hot, more like August
people crammed the nine block space
between where we were and the theater
we headed toward on 44th & Broadway

In L.A. someone brought in a 100 lb. Mk4
to detonate in cities across America—
the plan: to target as many as possible;

swept up by the crowd, the dizzying sound images
of clowning absurdity, a streaming billboard of people
brought to a sudden halt—

In New Mexico, birthplace of the Atom Bomb
a seven foot long warhead was transported in a van,
in N.Y.C., brought in a Nissan Pathfinder

metal barricades corralled a sprawling crowd
herded toward 8th Ave. no explanations as we
walked between police & fire trucks
rumors of kid's pranks, security for Ahmadinejad at the UN, etc.

across the country, a Cold War practice bomb
purchased on Craigslist and filled with poems
traveling at the speed of free thought
began exploding dissenting ideas

In N.Y.C. a propane type bomb meant to kill
as many as possible, failing to explode
smoked itself out in a car purchased

on Craigslist, setting off relief and fear

the other bomb" surfing across America..."
keeps growing more powerful

---
*Elsie The Poetry Bomb, April 2010

The New York Quarterly Foundation, Inc.
New York, New York

Poetry Magazine
Since 1969

Edgy, fresh, groundbreaking, eclectic—voices from all walks of life.

Definitely NOT your mama's poetry magazine!

The *New York Quarterly* has been defining the term contemporary American poetry since its first craft interview with W. H. Auden.

Interviews • Essays • and of course, lots of poems.

www.nyq.org

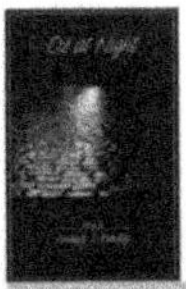

No contest! That's correct, NYQ Books are NO CONTEST to other small presses because we do not support ourselves through contests. Our books are carefully selected by invitation only, so you know that NYQ Books are produced with the same editorial integrity as the magazine that has brought you the most eclectic contemporary American poetry since 1969.

Books
www.nyq.org

poetry at the edge™

www.ingramcontent.com/pod-product-compliance
Lightning Source LLC
LaVergne TN
LVHW041339080426
835512LV00006B/538